Why Be Vegetarian

Debunking the excuses

Fee O'Shea

First Printing, 2014

Printed in the United States of America

ISBN-10: 1499751435

Liability Disclaimer

Why Be Vegetarian

Debunking the excuses

Introduction

Let me begin this introduction by pointing out what this book is NOT.

It is not a recipe book. There are literally millions of free vegetarian recipes on the internet. There are many vegetarian recipes books that you can find on the internet, and, I'm sure if you trot down to your local book store, you'll find beautiful vegetarian recipe books on the shelf filled with stunning, glossy photos to tempt your palate.

This book is not a "how to" book either, although there are some tips within the pages as I proceed to dispel any lingering doubts you may have.

What this book does do is what it says on the cover, debunk the excuse/s.

If you go through the Table of Contents, you'll see all the excuses known to this author and this book addresses those excuses in the hope that you will have a "aha moment".

I'll leave you now to get on with the reading.

Chapter 1:

Let's Begin With "What is A Vegetarian?"

Before I start to debunk your excuses I thought it is best to give you an understanding as to the meaning of all the different varieties of food groups:

Carnivore - Only eats meat, reserved more for the animal kingdom although I'm sure there are people out there who don't like veggies and would be more carnivore than anything else!

Omnivore - These people eat everything - red meat, white meat, fish, vegetables...MacD's, KFC, the list goes on...

Flexitarian - Supposedly a flexitarian eats vegetarian meals interspersed with meat. Could be mostly meat meals with the occasional vegetarian option or mainly vegetarian with the odd bit of meat thrown in for good measure - in other words a picky omnivore! More and more people, however, are becoming flexitarian as they have meatless days and this is a really good thing and the more flexitarians we have the better off the planet will be.

Pescetarian - A person whose "meat" choice is fish .... and I found this classification on the net "Vegaquarians or Fish-and-Chip-ocrits" which I thought suited well.

Pollo-vegetarians - Eats no red meat or fish, but does eat poultry.

Pollo-pescitarian - Add poultry to the fish and you have a pollo-pescitarian

Lacto vegetarians – Eats no meat, poulty or fish but does consume dairy but not eggs. (By dairy, I mean any milk or milk product that comes from any animal).

Ovo vegetarians - Eats no meat, poulty or fish and doesn't consume dairy products but does eat eggs.

Lacto-ovo vegetarians – These people don't eat beef, poultry, or fish, but do eat both eggs and dairy products. This is probably the most common Vegetarian as both eggs and cheese are the hardest things to give up.

Vegan - Does not eat anything that comes from an animal. A true vegan will also not use any animal product e.g. leather, wool etc.

Raw/living foodists – Vegan, these people eat at least 75% uncooked (items may be heated up to 105 degrees), unprocessed, organic fruits and vegetables, with the intention of preserving more vitamins and minerals. There are very few "pure" raw foodists though many people "eat raw" at least occasionally. It is recommended to have some raw foods each day even if it is only in the form of salads, nuts and fruits .... Raw foods are the most nutritious.

Fruitarians - Eats raw fruit and seeds only.

As you can see, there are all sorts of varieties of food groups

Most people will start out as a Flexitarian by reducing the amount of meat they consume. A lot will remove red meat from their diet first then the white meats and, usually, take out fish last. However, that is a generalization as there are also many who will cut all animal products out in one go.

My thoughts on cutting it all out in one go is that it is very hard to do. Being vegetarian is a "way of life". It is teaching yourself a completely new set of cooking and eating skills. So I always suggest that people start slowly and over time they will discover that cutting out meat hasn't been so bad at all.

Note: When I use the word "meat" I am referring to all animal/fish flesh. Also note that shellfish are included in the "meat". Molluscs and shellfish do not photosynthesise, therefore they are not plants. They are also able to escape from danger which indicates to me that they have enough of a brain and central nervous system to be aware of danger and interested in preserving their own lives.

It can also be difficult explaining to people your chosen food group. Many people think that a Vegetarian will also eat fish, although how they come to that conclusion with the word **VEGE-**tarian is beyond me.

If you are in the zone of "flexitarianism" then just say that you don't eat red meat (or chicken etc.), alternatively you can say that you don't eat meat but you do eat fish (or chicken etc.).

You can also use the word "flexitarian" if you are choosing to just have a meatless day or days per week. Meatless Mondays started during the war when food was rationed, however, there is a trend to bring this way of thinking back in order to ease the burden on the planet of raising live stock.

Once you have fully taken onboard the vegetarian eating, then you can say you're vegetarian (or vegan if you have removed dairy and eggs also).

14

Be prepared for questions as many people haven't got a clue. You will be asked things like:

"Oh, so you don't eat meat? ..... but you eat chicken (fish) right?"
"Why are you a vegetarian?"
"Aren't we meant to eat meat?"
"Don't you crave meat?"
"What do you eat for protein?"
"Aren't you worried about an iron deficiency?"
"If you're stranded on a desert island and the only thing there was meat, no greens – would you eat it?"
"Is this about animal rights?"
"Are you against leather?"
"Do you eat animal crackers?"

When you're in a restaurant you'll get asked:

"Is there anything in here that you can eat?"
"Shall we go somewhere else?"
"Don't you wish there was meat in that?"
"How can you have that without the bacon?"
"Is it o.k. if I eat this in front of you?"
"Oh look, they have French fries – you can eat that right?"

If you don't have the answers – don't worry, they probably wouldn't believe you anyway.

One easy way to get around situations or people who you think may not support you is to say that you have a bet with a friend that you can go a day/week/month without eating any animal product. You can then easily add "I thought it would be difficult, but I'm even surprising myself to how easy it is".

Turn the page and let's see if I can guess your excuse ......

Chapter 2:

I Would Be Vegetarian But ...

If you have purchased this book, then I'm guessing that you have, at least, considered the possibility of going vegetarian but maybe you just need to be convinced a little bit more that it is a good idea.

Most people in this situation have, what they think, is a very valid reason why they are dragging the chain and not making the commitment to give it a go.

As with most things, timing is everything and just the mere fact that you are reading this book tells me that the time is fast approaching that you want to try to have some vegetarian meals.

There are different reasons why people choose a vegetarian or vegan life. It could be because of economics, or health. Or, it could be about the welfare of animals or the sustainability of farming as we know it today.
This book is not about these issues, although I do touch on them a little. No, this book is about you and what stops you from taking that step.

Let's see if I can guess your reason. I'm sure it will be one of the following (if not several).

The conversation usually starts with "I would be vegetarian but....

- it's too hard.

- my husband/wife/partner/son/daughter (have I missed anyone), won't.

- animals are meant to be eaten.

- I need meat for protein ..... *or insert vitamins/mineral or any other nutritional adjective you would like to use.*

- if everyone went vegetarian – what would happen to those billions of animals?

- I really like ...... *insert favorite meat e.g. ribs/steak/chicken wings/fish.*

- plants have feelings too.

- cavemen ate meat.

- lions kill animals.
- it won't make a difference, I'm just one person.

- we are at the top of the food chain.

- I'd rather focus on helping people than animals.

- I know farmers who really love their animals.

- I'm into ..... *insert a sport e.g. body building/athletics* .... so I need the meat

- vegetarian involves weird fake meat.

Have I missed anything out? I'm quite sure you'll be the first to let me know if I did. So what I propose to do now is start to answer these questions.

The next chapter will concentrate on THE most common excuse – "It's too hard".

So read on, my friend, hopefully by the end of book I'll have you convinced to give it a try.

Chapter 3:

Becoming Vegetarian ... It's Too Hard.

This is the most common excuse there is. When I was vegetarian, (I am now vegan), people usually asked me "isn't it hard?" which, naturally, I responded "no". However, they still use this when on the flip side they tell me that they would like to be vegetarian the excuse is: "it's too hard" – I do wonder about their thought pattern!

I wish I had a dollar for every time some-one has said to me "I would really like to be vegetarian, but I just don't know what I'd cook." Or "I would be vegetarian, but I don't do the cooking in my family."

I can understand, in some ways, this seems to be a good excuse. It can be a bit daunting to try and get your head around a new way of cooking, and, if you are not the cook, then that could be a bit more challenging.

So let's look at these two different aspects.

If you are the cook.

We become so used to the way we prepare food that to have to start dishing up two separate meals can be quite taxing – or so it may seem. Hence the reason a lot of cooks will use the excuse that it is just too hard.

Nothing could be further from the truth.

A great trick is to have individual dishes containing a variety of foods that everyone can then help themselves to. This could, in fact, be quite a novel and fun way because I do know a lot of people dish up the meal straight onto the plates and hand them out.

Just think for a moment how great it would be to have all the food out on the table so everyone can sit around, choose what they want and fill their own plates. Not only are you giving your family choices, but you are also creating a wonderful environment around the table to share conversation.

Yes, you will have more dishes and, yes, you will have to set the table. But think of the advantages especially bringing your family together even if it is for only one meal a day.

Besides, the food that remains can be put together, (if they go together), into one bowl, covered and put into the fridge to be used for either lunch the next day or incorporated into tomorrow night's dinner.

Here's one way - cook your vegetarian dishes and add a plate of meat onto the table. *Or* .... If you're cooking a stew - then prepare the stock with veggies all minus the meat, prepare the meat as usual in a separate pot then place some of the stew stock over to continue cooking as normal. (yes, you will need to work with two pots, but one can be small). The stew stock without the meat you can add beans or lentils or chickpeas. Then, voila, you have the meat stew for them and a vegetarian stew for you. It's all just a matter of thinking outside the square.

Being the cook does give you carte blanch in the kitchen. I've known people who have just not added meat dishes on their vegetarian days. One woman told me that she had told the meat eaters that they could get their own meals if they didn't want to eat what she had prepared. It, apparently, took two weeks before the rest of the family were tired of that and joined her at the table with the vegetarian food. The irony is that they really loved what she was making.

Of course you probably will get teased a bit .... But that will soon go away and it may surprise you that the other will start liking your food!!

If you're not the cook.

If you don't have control in the kitchen then you are going to have to sit down with the cook and talk.

A good idea is to start slowly. Say that you'd like to have more vegetarian foods and offer to either, do the cooking of them or provide the recipes.
Make sure you lay some ground rules – like, I won't disrespect your choice to eat meat, if you respect my choice of being vegetarian.

Make sure that you have good, nutritious food and if you help with the preparing of it I'm sure that will go a long way to having a great relationship with whoever is the cook.

You could suggest the idea of different dishes, (as suggested above), with the meat on a separate dish giving you the option of choosing.

Where it does become a little more labor intensive for a meat-eating cook is when a dish like the stew, has to be separated. This is when you can offer to cook your own.

Again, think outside the square and make sure that you don't disrespect the meat eaters in the family. Oh, and being vegetarian means you don't disrespect animals either as we'll discuss in the next chapter.

Chapter 4:

Animals Are Meant To Be Eaten ... You Really Think So?

The funnier way that I've heard this sentence is: "If animals are not meant to be eaten, then why are they made of meat?"
Mmmmm, how to answer. Think about it – humans are made of meat, but you don't eat them ..... or ...... do you???

So let's take this opportunity to talk about the animals.

The problem is that we have two kinds of domestic animals –

1. The pet

2. The food.

and both live extraordinarily different lives.

Now in actual fact, there is absolutely no difference between the animal who is bred for being your pet and the animal who is bred for being your food.

All animals are really not so different to the human animal. Dogs, cats, cows, pigs and all other animals clearly show affection to one another. They also show happiness as well as fear and all have the absolute desire to live. We also know that animals have pain receptors – if an animal is being hurt, it is feeling exactly what you would be feeling if it was you.

These animals are living, breathing, feeling sentient beings who, just like you, want to live their lives the way they are meant to.

With your pet …. I'm sure you would not:

- Allow it to live in a confined space where it could not turn around.
- Castrate it without anaesthetic.
- Remove its tail without anaesthetic.
- Confine it to a cage so its kittens or puppies could not be looked after properly.

(I could add a lot more bullet points here as to what happens to farm animals but just go online and Google "treatment of farm animals facts" you will find videos and articles and images galore).

And, I'm sure that when the time came you certainly would not truck it off to get slaughtered.

Paul McCartney is quoted as saying:

"If slaughter houses had glass walls we would not eat meat."

Animals become frantic as they watch the animal before them in the killing-line being prodded, beaten, electrocuted, and knifed. There are many, many times that the animal is not even dead before it reaches the skinning part. There are many animals who back up into the truck as they can smell the death and are well aware of what is going to happen to them. But doing this only makes the humans more violent towards them and they are prodded with electric prods ... think "taser" – difference is, this animal is not a criminal.

But it starts way before the animals get to the abattoirs.

The intensive production of animals has created a "factory" type farming system for your pork, chicken and beef .... We can also add dairy cows under that "beef" heading as dairy cows are also being intensely farmed with little or no regard for the welfare of animal.

Beef:

The calf is left with its mother until around 6 – 8 months of age. Bull calves are castrated with no anesthetic and kept until they have gained the desired weight before being shipped off to be slaughtered. Female calves are usually kept and once they reach sexual maturity (15 months) they are then inseminated delivering their calf 9 months later. Female cows (heifers) are re-bred each 12 months. They continue until they are no longer able to breed, (around 7 to 9 years), then slaughtered.

Males calves from the dairy industry have a very short life. They are taken from their mothers in as little as a few hours from birth and, as there is no money in male calves, many are killed on the farm. Many are conscious when their throat is slit due to inadequate stunning or are they are just brutally hammered to death with a blunt object.

Mother cows can be heard bellowing out wildly trying to find their babies as well as running after the cattle trucks that take their babies to separate farms or abattoirs.

Pigs:

Piglets are castrated with no anesthetic at a few days old and live their lives packed in sheds with no chance to express natural behaviors such as digging and nesting. Tail docking (again without anesthetic) is routine to prevent the pigs from biting each other's tails in frustration. Pregnant pigs are confined to sow stalls, with not even enough room to turn around. The sows are supplied no bedding and are often seen biting the bars of the stall or swaying repetitively. *Note: Not all countries have the pigs confined during all the pregnancy, however, they are usually are confined for the first months.*

Just prior to birthing, the pigs are shifted into farrowing crates, pretty much the same as sow stalls or crates. Not much room at all. After the birth the mother can really do nothing to look after her babies other than lie down to feed

Chickens

Chickens raised for meat are known as broilers and are raised in sheds containing as many as 45,000 birds. They grow unnaturally fast due to selective breeding and antibiotics pumped into their food. Chickens have a natural lifespan of 10-15 years but broilers are decapitated at 6-7 weeks.

In egg production hens are confined to cages giving each bird about an A4 piece of paper of personal space. The birds suffer broken bones, feather loss and skin abrasions because of a lifetime confined to a tiny wire cage. Often their beaks are seared off (no anesthetic) with a hot blade to prevent them pecking at each other from stress and many hens develop osteoporosis because they are artificially pushed to produce many more eggs than in natural conditions.

Chickens, when hatched, are checked for their sex. Males get thrown alive into a grinder as they are not needed. Even the "free range" sector has a lot to answer for. Their chickens may "run free", however, you can guarantee that they have acquired the laying hens through companies employing the sexing method above. Also, these farmers face the same problem as caged hen farmers – what to do with the chicken when it stops laying.

A chicken can live around 10-15 years, however, their laying ability (especially in the commercial sector) is only about 2 years. These "free range" farmers can't afford to keep their chickens past the laying age......need I say more?

Free range meat does not necessarily mean the life of the animal is perfect. Cows can be de-horned and pigs can be castrated and painful rings put through their nose. You have to re-member that free range is still farming and the farmer does have to make a living.

Yes, the animals do have a better life, but their death is just the same. In fact, some argue that the factory animal at least has just a short life al-beit brutal, while the free range animal lives for longer and happier but at the end of it endures pain and anguish that is probably far worse.

Before we end this chapter I would also like to tell you a little about "organic".
Meat that is labeled organic does not mean that the animal has had a good life. Usually far from it. All that it means is that the animal has been fed organic food and not been subjected to anti-biotics, hormones or an arsenic-based additive as many non-organic chicken products do.

The animals are still raised in barns or confined spaces. The downside is that, because they don't get the anti-biotics, these animals can have all sorts of illness, have a higher mortality rate and be subjected to even more parasites than their drugged counterparts.

So, the idea of free range and organic as being the ideal meat to have is brought about by the happy chicken, well fed cow and cute piggy that is portrayed on packaging giving the illusion of well cared for animals. Don't buy into it. It is not necessarily the reality.

If you want more information on any animal farming methods then search the internet, however, make sure you do a good search – read up on both sides of the arguments and come to your own conclusion. Be prepared for some very shocking and gruesome photos and videos.

Chapter 5:

I Need Meat To Balance My Diet ... Now who told you that?

I'm going to go out on a limb here and say that where you've heard that from goes way back, even probably before your time. Chances are you've grown up with the idea that meat is an integral part of what must be present in the diet in order to maintain a balanced diet ... perhaps not quite in those words, but close enough.

This has come from the meat industry.

That's right. This is business. Nothing to do with your health at all. The meat industry has been bombarding us with this notion for years.

From the 1950s to present day the marketing campaigns have increased as we saw the growth of radio, television and the internet.

Back in 1992 the "Beef, it's what's for dinner" campaign really started the intensive push for you to purchase beef. This slogan has changed over the years - "Beef. It's what you want", to the present "Discover the Power of Protein in the Land of Lean Beef" and even teaming up with the Dairy industry in 1993 to create the "Double Cheese Cheeseburger Days" campaign.

Beef is not the only meat to have hard hitting campaigns. In 1987 pork came out with an aggressive campaign "The Other White Meat". This was to get consumers buying more and their advertising said that pork is as tasty, nutritious and versatile as any other meal.

Chicken used to be a real luxury until around the 1980's when it became a popular idea that chicken was healthier than red meat.
Back in the 1950's it took up to four months for a chicken to get plump enough for the table, hence the reason it was regarded as a delicacy.

However, now, chickens are churned out at such a rate it is fast becoming the most popular meat .... Healthy? Put it this way, the chicken of today has been especially genetically engineered to go from hatching to dispatching in 35-39 days. My personal opinion is: *that just is not normal.*

Marketing campaigns are all about getting you, the consumer, to buy more. They are there to get you to believe that meat is healthy, that you should eat it and that there is no other way to get your nutrition.

So now that you understand that it's been more about the industries' need to make a profit and less about the industries' concern about your health that we can now look a bit more subjectively about meat.

You've certainly heard the expression many times, "You are what you eat." Have you ever really thought about what it means? And do you think about it when you're making food choices?

In some ways, we do become what we eat, literally. Have you ever seen an example of your blood plasma after eating a fast food hamburger? What was previously a clear liquid becomes cloudy with the fat and cholesterol that's absorbed from eating a high-fat hamburger.

And when you think about it, we also become what we don't eat. When we switch from eating meat to a vegetarian-based diet, we can lose that excess fat, are less prone to many types of cancers. Our cholesterol can improve. When we're leaner and eating fewer animal products, then many other health and fitness issues are reduced. The incidence of Type II diabetes is reduced. Blood pressure falls into normal ranges. When you're healthier, you're taking fewer medications. Even if you have a prescription drug benefit in your health plan, you're still saving money with fewer co-payments on medications.

If you have a family history of high cholesterol or high blood pressure, then it's particularly incumbent on you to revise your eating habits. Moving towards a more vegetarian diet has been shown statistically to reduce the incidence of so many of the diseases of industrialized countries. Vegetarians are statistically healthier than omnivorous persons; they're leaner and live longer.

Isn't it time to think about what you want to be and to eat accordingly? People on a diet of mainly meat, (especially those consuming processed meat), tend to be sluggish and over-weight. Do you want the health risk that goes with eating animal products, with their high fat content? Vegetarians, especially those who have limited dairy and eggs, are generally leaner and fitter with a longer anticipated lifespan. It's never too late to change what you're doing and increase your chances for a longer, fitter life.

However, you must still make sure that you have a balanced diet. There are a number of vegetarians who really don't look after themselves as well as they should. So the more restrictive you become with your diet the more you will need to educate yourself to be sure you're getting all the necessary proteins and vitamins that you need to maintain good health, especially muscle and heart health.

If, on the other hand, you embrace the huge array of vegetarian foods (so many more possibilities than there are with meat), you will have a wonderfully balanced diet and you won't have to concern yourself with "am I getting enough ..... *insert the protein/mineral/vitamin of your choice*

The next chapter is a fair doozie of a subject to tackle and one that I get told a lot ..... they don't expect the answer I give either!

Chapter 6:

But I Like The Taste of Meat ... What if I said you didn't have to give up meat entirely?

We are brought up on meat ... all kinds of meat, from beef to chicken, from pork to fish we have basically four types of meat to choose from.

Of course there are the hunters who add to their meat with game, from venison to wild boar, from duck to swordfish.

And so it is very natural for you to believe that you will miss the bacon and the steaks, the hamburgers and the barbequed sausages, the fried chicken wings and grilled lamb.

However, going vegetarian is a journey. And, like all journeys, it has a starting point. The starting point on this journey is to have one meat free day a week. Yes, that's it, just one meat free day. And if you really want to embrace the movement, you could in fact make it a total animal product free day which means you don't have dairy or eggs either.

Hard to do? No way. Here is one day, just one day that you could slot into your meat-eating life once a week.

Breakfast:

(I've even given you an either/or, of course you can have the lot if you wish.)

Either – start the day with a Smoothie. Into a food processor or blender place about 3 cups of chopped fruit (bananas, strawberries, or whatever fruit is in season), 2 Tblsp of oatmeal and about 2 1/2 cups of coconut or soy yoghurt (or about ½ that amount if just plain coconut/soy milk), combine until creamy, pour into glasses and serve. To gain maximum benefit prepare the fruit just before using.

Or – Muesli: You can either choose commercially made muesli *note: check label for animal free ingredients,* or make it yourself which gives you total control over the ingredients.
Mix up: 1 ½ cups of rolled oats, 3 Tblsp gound linseed (also known as flax seed), 2 cups of mixed nuts and seeds of your choice. In saucepan heat 2 large Tblsp margerine or butter alternative and

3 large Tblsp crunchy peanut butter until melted and mix.

Put the dry ingredients into a roasting pan and mix through the "butter" mixture. Bake in pre-heated oven 160C/325F for about 15 minutes turning the mixture every 5 minutes. Should be golden. Serve with your choice of fresh fruits and dairy free milk.

Lunch:

This is generally easy as it can be as simple as creating a sandwich filled with salad type vegetables. In the winter, you may consider making a vegetable soup.

Dinner:

Dinnertime is usually where meat eaters get stuck. They think along the lines of what they should "replace" the meat with. Sometimes, this is one way to think, but if you are serious about creating lovely meat free meals, then decide that you will choose an ingredient or two and create a meal around that ingredient.

For example: Choose to cook with lentils. Now, go to your fridge and see what vegetables you have. Maybe you have a pumpkin. Head to the computer, type into Google: vegetarian lentils pumpkin. Make sure to add the word "vegetarian" or even "vegan" for completely animal free. Take a look at the photo below – and this is only the first 6 there are literally pages and pages of recipes!

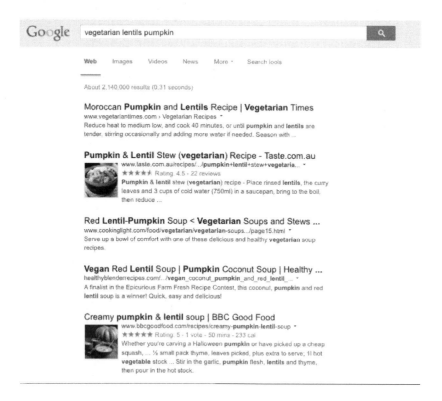

Instead of the lentils you can use, tofu, chickpeas or any type of bean. I've even given you a few recipes with the free book (*access to this book is near the last page*), so there should be no excuse ☺

The next excuse is just bizarre!

Chapter 7:

If Everyone Went Vegetarian What Would Happen To All The Animals? ...What do you think would happen?

This particular excuse always amuses me. This chapter will be short, because this is totally illogical thinking.

1.   Everyone will not go vegetarian all at once. What on earth makes you think that they will? This is the human race we're talking about – fickle, stubborn, greedy and so many can't even be kind to other humans let alone animals.

Who was it that said:
"You can't please all the people all of the time" ?
– well you're certainly not going to change everyone's mind all at once.

2.   As the demand for meat diminishes, so will the production of the farmed animals. They will just get less and less. Of course, I do not expect to see a huge reduction in my lifetime and proba-

bly not in yours either, but maybe the new generation that's coming now will start to see the changes.

Let's remove the words "to all the animals" from the title of this chapter and just ask – If everyone went vegetarian what would happen?

•   The first thing would be a dramatic change, for the better, to our environment.
You only need less than ½ an acre of land on a vegetarian diet versus 2 acres of land for a meat eater (per year.).

It takes 2,500 gallons of water to produce one pound of beef but it takes only 25 gallons of water to produce one pound of wheat.

A lot of the destruction of the rain forest would cease. Fast food causes more destruction than you think as massive herds of cattle just graze the land until it's completely useless then more rain forest is cut down to provide food. Even in countries like the USA, Europe, Australia and N.Z. where there is a beef and dairy industry, topsoil erosion is a real problem.

Fertilizers used in feed crops produce potent greenhouse gases along with methane gas from cattle and farmers who burn fossil fuels for heating and cooling of the huge farm factory buildings.

All these things have a huge impact on our environment and are not sustainable.

•   The world going vegetarian would also reduce world hunger. Big statement – absolute fact.

At the moment, we do have enough food to go round. However, even though we produce enough to feed all 7 billion people, those who do go hungry either do not have the land to grow food or money to buy it.

It is projected that by 2050 the world population will reach 9.6 billion people. This is now where we look at the logistics of how we use the land – it simply will not be viable to have a meat driven population.

It takes up to 13 pounds of grain to produce 1 pound of meat.
13 pounds of grain would feed a village instead of just one family.
At present, 27% of calories come from animal products and 1.4 billion people are starving.
If people reduced those calories down to 10% there would be no starving people at all.
This is because it takes 1 acre of land to raise cattle for 20 pounds of meat. Use that same 1 acre and you could grow 365 pounds of protein rich soy beans and 17 times more people could be saved from starvation.

Of the 145 million tons of grain and soy fed to livestock, only 21 million tons of meat and by-products are used. The waste is 124 million tons per year at a value of 20 billion US dollars. It has been calculated that this sum would feed, clothe and house the world's entire population for one year.

•   We really have to stop trying to change the eating habits of other countries – it's not going to do the world any favors.

There are still countries, especially in Asia, that are primarily vegetarian and India would probably be the number 1 vegetarian country in the world. However, with the western style of eating meat (mainly the fast food industry), fast becoming popular it means that the demand for meat is growing. Again, not sustainable for our planet.

So there you have it. Yes, in an ideal world, we would all be much more "health of the planet" conscious, but, while there is money to be made ...... it's not going to happen. However, you can do your little bit by choosing a vegetarian lifestyle.

And, speaking of health, that segues nicely into the next chapter.

Chapter 8:

Meat Is A Key Source Of ___ (fill in the blank with Protein, vitamins, minerals) ... ah but is it?

I really should direct you back to chapter 5 as it's pretty much of a muchness, (and, yes, I know there's no such word as muchness, but it sounds good!).

Another one of those questions that I get asked a lot is "what do you do for protein?" My answer is "same as you, eat food."

So let's look at protein, and the same will apply for all other vitamins and minerals.

For some unfathomable reason people have a fixation on where Vegetarians get their protein from. It's usually the first question that you will be asked when you say "I'm Vegetarian". This happens more with "I'm Vegan".

And, I'm assuming that if you are wanting to switch to a vegetarian lifestyle, you'll be thinking the exact same thing.

Conventional thinking says that protein is obtained from meat, fish, eggs, milk and dairy products such as cheese. These all contain complete proteins that contain all the essential amino acids that are needed for the human body. So it is correct that these foods do have protein.

However, meat eaters have too much protein as they are also getting protein from plant sources which they are usually unaware of.

Protein is found in many vegetable sources. Some of these vegetable proteins are complete in that they contain all the essential amino acids just like animal protein. Others are incomplete and must be combined together to produce a complete protein that the body can use.

Most plant foods contain some protein. A vegetarian who eats a wide variety of foods will consume sufficient and correct protein in the course of day.

A very simplistic way of looking at new research shows that the different proteins will be stored in the body until their matching protein comes along. See, you really don't have to worry, just eat a variety of food and your body will take care of the details!

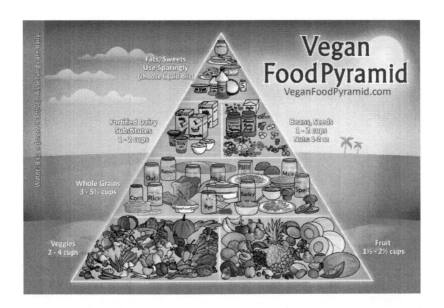

Note: *I have used the Vegan food pyramid, if you do include eggs and dairy in your diet, remember to do so in moderation.*

Nuts and seeds are an under appreciated source of protein. They can be added to a wide range of sweet and savory vegetarian dishes.

Soya beans are a source of complete protein and for that reason soya products are an important part of a vegetarian diet. Commercially manufactured soya based meat substitutes are now widely available in supermarkets. They come in variety of forms and are often made into pies, burgers, sausages and other ready prepared products that offer the busy vegetarian a convenience food.
In saying that, I am not a believer in processed foods vegetarian or otherwise.

Tofu is a great food that you can do so much with from savory to sweet foods, you can even use it to make a delicious mayonnaise.

Soya milk can be found in most chiller cabinets next to the cows' milk, or it can be found on the shelf with other UHT milks. You will also find soya yoghurts and soya cheeses. **Note:** *not all supermarkets carry these types of products and you may have to look in health shops or organic stores.*

Another meat substitute is mycoprotein which is made from a variety of fungus. Like soya protein it is sold in various forms that can be used in a range of recipes. You will also find it in ready made products often sold under the brand name "Quorn." **Note:** *Quorn does use egg, so not suitable if going without dairy and eggs as well.*

But, let's get back to "home cooking". Beans, peas and lentils, known collectively as pulse, make up one of the major sources of protein for a Vegetarian. Even though they are not a complete protein in themselves, because you will be adding other ingredients/foods to your plate, you will find that you do, in fact, have the right and enough protein for the day.

I really don't think about how much "protein" or anything else for that matter I'm getting. I just make sure that my daily and weekly meals are varied, well balanced, tasty and look good – nutrition is already there.

So here is what I mean about balance. I use all sorts of foods - beans, lentils, quinoa, chickpeas, veggies, raw foods, tofu, nutritional yeast - very little wheat, very little sugar (use dates a lot), and good vegan chocolate of course!

I use spelt, chickpea or quinoa flours and nuts, seeds, herbs and spices. My salads are usually made from micro-greens which I grow myself ..... you will find how to grow them very easily on my website www.thevegetariancenter.com

To my salad I add ground nuts, seeds, edible flowers, herbs along with normal salad vegetables.

My dinner:
Veggie pie with lentil base, mashed potatoes, spinach and salad. A very "normal" meal.

Another absolute bonus is Google – I just love

Google as it is a wealth of information and inspiration. Just typing in an ingredient and the word vegetarian or vegan ... it's amazing what recipes come up.

Really, the point is, please don't stress about how much protein or vitamins you are having. As long as you follow the basics of balance you will be fine.

I do not recommend taking supplements, however, this does depend on your general health and I do suggest you talk with your Doctor and perhaps have blood tests done once a year, (more so if you are totally Vegan).

The two main vitamins that can be of concern are Vitamin D and Vitamin B12.

If you do not get enough safe sun exposure then you definitely need to purchase products that have "fortified Vitamin D", e.g. cereals and soy products. Surprisingly enough, certain mushrooms have vitamin D! If this is not an option, then perhaps you can look at a supplement.

The "B" vitamins are widely distributed throughout the vegetable food range so, if you are having a balanced diet, there will be no reason for you to be concerned as you will be getting enough of this as well as all the other vitamins and minerals you need.

Vitamin B12 only occurs naturally in animal products, so a Vegan should look at purchasing fortified foods or taking a supplement.

As a Vegan I do have a blood test at the beginning of each year to check my health. I am happy to report that my iron levels are "better than a meat-eater" – my Doctor's words, not mine, my calcium levels are great – much to his surprise and my cholestrol and blood pressure perfectly normal.

There are even some insurance companies who will give a discount to vegetarians!

Chapter 9:

I Don't Want To Be Left Out ... This I can understand.

Strange as it may seem to you, this is one excuse that I can relate to. However, it's not an excuse that I agree with as there really is no reason why you should be "left out" from anything.

Therefore, even though the excuse is not so bizarre, it certainly has no basis to sustain a good argument for not going vegetarian.

The only times that you think you may feel "left out" are times associated around social dining. If this is the case, then it begs the question – How many times to you actually eat out at places that do not have a vegetarian option?

So, for argument's sake, let's assume your social life rules your dining existence and we will go through some scenarios.

1. BBQ. This, possibly, is the most difficult for new vegetarians to handle especially if you live in a strong meat eating area, (parts

of the USA, Australia and New Zealand spring to mind).

The BBQ is generally an event that you are invited to, therefore you will know your host. Here's what you do. You get in touch with your host, say you are currently doing the vegetarian thing as an experiment and that you will bring your own food to put on the BBQ, (that way you won't get ribbed – *get the pun?* – or get laughed at).

This is the time that the pre-made "fake" meat sausages and patties really come in handy. It is far easier to get them at the supermarket than to try and make them yourself, plus the pre-made ones hold together better.

There is the issue of sharing the grill of the BBQ with the meat, meaning cross contamination. To overcome this you can precook your sausages/patties at home, wrap them in aluminum foil and put that onto the grill to heat up.

There are usually plenty of salad dishes and breads served as well as wonderful deserts. Of course, you can also contribute to the meal by bringing something extra so I'm sure you certainly won't go hungry.

For a Vegan, it can be a little more difficult, however, I'm not about to tackle that in this book as this is about vegetarianism.

2. You are invited to a friend's home for dinner. This really is a no-brainer. The operative word here is "friend". You just talk to your friend and if s/he is concerned about what to serve you, then offer to bring a vegetarian dish for everyone to share. Do ask your friend, though, to not incorporate meat into some of the side dishes.

3. Restaurants. The 21st century is wonderful and modern in most parts of the world so this really should not be a problem at all. Most restaurants will offer a vegetarian option. However, there are still some who are behind the eight ball and simply do not understand that they are turning away business if they don't.

   You have the choice if you wish to dine at a restaurant. Steer clear of places that do not have a vegetarian option of at least two choices. What this tells me is that the chef is stuck in the past and probably not very good.

   Checking the menu online before going out makes it easier, or if you are strolling the eating district most restaurants have their menu at the door so you can look before going in.

If it's a work do and you have no choice of restaurant, then ring them ahead of time and talk to them about the vegetarian options. You will find that most places are only too happy to cater for you.

4. Cafes. This is pretty much the same as restaurants above. If it is the "cabinet food" you are after for a quick lunch, you always have the option of being decadent and going to the delicious cakes and cookies.

The above are the only scenarios I can think where you may strike a glitch. I have been to restaurants in the past where there has been no vegetarian option, or only one that I don't want, and I have asked the waitress if it is possible to mix ingredients from two or three different dishes.

There has never been an issue doing that, in fact, my plate ends up looking and tasting awesome and the meat eaters at the table wished they had ordered what I'd got!

It's something that I continue to do as a Vegan and I still end up with delicious "mixed meals". I've also found that a great chef can get really creative and enjoy the challenge.

Of course you do have to deal with Holidays. Will you be away for Christmas, home for Thanksgiving with friends for Halloween?

The next chapter is going to cover the holidays, but there are also tips in there that you will be able to use for any time you want to entertain.

Chapter 10:

What About The Holidays? ... Good question.

If you are having family and/or friends over to celebrate the holidays, the first thing you will need to decide on is whether you are going to make the meal entirely vegetarian or if you are going to cater for the meat eaters in the group.

Let's assume you are going to make it entirely vegetarian.

Planning a beautiful, yet nutrient-dense, delicious holiday meal for both your meat eating and vegetarian guests can be a little daunting at first, but it can also bring out your creativity! Many side dishes you make can be easily made vegetarian, with little difference in taste.

The first step in planning accordingly would be to find out which of your guests are vegetarian, and what kind of vegetarian they are. Do they eat eggs or cheese? If so, you'll have a few more possibilities. If they don't, that's okay, you'll still have plenty of options to work with.

If you're new to the vegetarian lifestyle and are lucky enough to have vegetarian guests coming, then ask for some input or help from them. They may have some great recipe ideas, shortcuts, or simple tricks of the trade they can share with you to make your holiday meal preparation go smoothly.

For instance, you can substitute vegetable broth for chicken broth, or simply leave the meat or meat drippings out of vegetables and soups. This will also cut down on the fat content.

A great tip is to place different dishes with different foods on the table so your guests can choose what they want. That covers those who are vegan or have other food preferences. Funnily enough, you will find that the meat eaters will eat everything ..... and love it!

Most importantly, keep in mind that the holidays are about peace, love, and understanding. With this in mind, please try not to be judgmental of what people you love choose to eat. If you do have other vegetarians/vegans around your table then seize the opportunity to learn from them. Incorporate their ideas into your own to ensure your family is eating a variety nutrient-dense, delicious fruits, vegetables, grains, seeds, and nuts at every meal.

Let's say the annual 4th of July cookout is quickly

approaching. Whether you're expecting vegetarian guests, you've newly transitioned to vegetarianism yourself, or you'd just like to incorporate more meatless recipes to give some variety to your cookout menu, there are all kind of ways to prepare meatless options.

Before beginning, remember that most vegetarian foods are more fragile than meat, and do not contain as much fat. Therefore, clean and well-lubricated grill is essential to successfully grilling vegetables. It'd be a shame for those beautifully grilled peppers to stick to the grill!

Traditionally, vegetables have been considered a side dish in most meals, but at a cookout they can take center stage as the entrée. Almost any kind of vegetable is great for grilling. Complement your meal by serving them over pasta, rice or polenta.

You can also make them into extraordinary sandwiches with a soy-based cheese and some freshly baked rolls or bread. Cut the vegetables lengthwise into thin slices in the case of zucchini and eggplant, or into thick rings, in the case of onions, tomatoes and peppers. If you'd rather have your veggies in handy bite-size pieces for serving with pasta and the like, try using a special pan for the grill with small holes that keep the veggies from falling through the grill and being lost. And probably the easiest way to grill vegetables on the grill is shish-ka-bob style!

This is a time when you can use the pre-made vegetarian sausages, Chicken-free nuggets or mock meats. You could even try making your own chickpea and lentil patties.

Don't forget to balance out those grilled vegetables with some fresh fruit salads, perfectly chilled and juicy. Watermelon, strawberries, grapes, and citrus fruits all complement one another well in a delightful fruit salad prepared with non-dairy whipped cream. Also use fruits to experiment with some fun smoothies and slushies for the kids – they're fun and better for them than sugary sodas.

Christmas is a season of peace, love and harmony. It's a time that brings families and friends together to reconnect and find comfort and happiness being together. It's also about respect for fellow man, appreciating and embracing one another's differences.

Take some time over the holiday season to reflect on the reasons for your choice to become vegetarian, and enforce your commitment and dedication to the vegetarian lifestyle. What reason, or reasons, helped you decide that vegetarianism was the right choice for you?

Was it Economic? A meat-based diet can be very

expensive. Fresh produce bought in season can be very affordable, and can be prepared (dried, canned, frozen) so that it can be enjoyed later in the season.

Was it Ethical? Did you choose not to eat meat because of the meat processing techniques are incredibly cruel to animals? Do some research on the internet or the library, visit the PETA website or other animal welfare websites, and you're very likely to find more credible reasoning that affirms your choice.

Was it Environmental? A vegetarian lifestyle is more environmentally friendly – large ranching operations cause topsoil erosion, coyotes and other natural predators are destroyed routinely to protect herds of cows which are only slaughtered anyway later on, and commercial fishing operations are damaging the ocean's ecosystems.

Was it to Improve Your Health? Eating a vegetarian diet has been shown to be a very healthy lifestyle, as it helps fight heart disease, reduces cancer risks, lowers cholesterol, helps lower blood sugar and reverse the effects of diabetes, lowers the obesity risk, and reduces the risk of osteoporosis, as meat consumption has been shown to promote bone loss.

And remember: just because it's Christmas, it doesn't mean you can't enjoy many of the same wonderful holiday treats you've become accustomed to, as long as they are prepared with your vegetarian lifestyle in mind. Breads and cookies prepared with vegetable shortening, egg substitutes (if vegan), whole grain flours and soymilks as well as numerous choices for vegetable dishes and salads can all be enjoyed by both vegetarians and non-vegetarians alike during the holiday! So remember the reason for the season, reaffirm your reasoning for your life choice, and be proud of it, and of yourself.

If you're hosting Thanksgiving at your house and are expecting vegetarian guests this year, don't worry about preparing one large meat eating meal, and another separate vegetarian meal. Most vegetarians do not require a 'meat equivalent' at Thanksgiving.

Yes, traditionally, Thanksgiving is largely about the food. But more importantly it's about family, togetherness, happiness and peace. If this is your first Thanksgiving after transitioning to a vegetarian lifestyle, try some of these ideas to incorporate healthy food preparation into your meal that your vegetarian guests, and you as host, will be thankful for this Thanksgiving:

- If you are going to have a turkey then bake some stuffing outside of the turkey to put with your vegetarian option.

- Make the gravy vegetarian.

- Keep cooking utensils separate to prevent "cross-contamination" between meat foods and vegetarian foods.

- Use vegetable oils instead of animal fats for frying, and vegetable shortening like Crisco for pie crust.

- Read ingredients lists carefully on pre-packaged foods, being aware of terms like gelatin, whey, and "natural flavors" that can be animal-derived.

- Have bowls of chutneys, pestos, sauces and other condiments for people to help themselves to.

- Offer plenty of breads, beverages, fresh fruits, and non-gelatin desserts, which are suitable without modification for most vegetarians.

- You could try preparing a "Tofurky" or a vegetarian turkey equivalent especially if there are other vegetarians coming. Your meat-eating guests might just be curious enough to want to try it!

- Ask your vegetarian guest for help, tips, or recipes that would complement the vegetarian choice. You may find that your guest offers to help out in the kitchen or bring a dish from home. Please don't take this as an insult to your cooking; take it as a desire to share traditions at Thanksgiving. Even meat-eating homes can benefit from a healthy, nutrient-dense vegetarian recipe idea any time of the year!

- Most importantly – make TONS of new, delicious (not overly cooked) vegetables that are perfectly in season like squashes, sweet potatoes, and green beans, etc.

- And have lots of different, interesting dishes using pulses, nuts and seeds on your table for your guests to help themselves to.

These ideas can be incorporated into any celebration, holiday or just having friends over for dinner. It can be such fun – you just need to get a little creative. Search the internet for ideas.

If you are invited out for holiday celebrations then just use the ideas in the previous chapter.

The next chapter is a bit of fun.

Chapter 11:

Some of The Other Excuses ....

"My Husband (*fill in the person*) Wont"

"I would really like to be vegetarian, but my husband/partner etc would never support me" . This is usually followed by "and I don't really want to be making two meals".

I don't know how many times I've talked to people who say that they'd really like to be vegetarian but the rest of the family want to keep eating meat.

In my mind this is a really lame excuse, especially if it comes from the main cook of the family. If, however, it's the other way round and it's not coming from the actual cook, then it can be a little more difficult ..... but certainly not a reason to continue eating meat.

So I'll refer you back to chapter 3

"I know farmers who really love their animals."

So do I, but no matter how much they love them, these animals still end up in the slaughter houses. These are still farmed animals and are treated as a commodity. Even if your friend the farmer treats them well, I'll bet he doesn't treat them the same as you treat your pet cat or dog.

Does your farmer friend use anesthetic when castrating or tail docking?

Does your farmer friend take young calves or piglets away from their mothers within a period of a few hours to about 20 days old?

Now I can hear you say, yes but, cows (*insert pigs or chickens*) are different to my dog/cat. Hate to burst your bubble, but no, they are not.

In fact, it is documented that pigs are more intelligent than dogs or even young children and yet they are farmed, most times in horrendous conditions, and end up as the bacon, ham and pork you enjoy eating.

It's well documented that all farmed animals, when allowed to live a natural life, are feeling individuals who have natural needs and desires.

At the end of the day, there is no such thing as humane killing.

"I'm into sport"

So are:

Fiona Oakes - vegan all her adult life broke three marathon World Records in 2013 & is now the fastest female to run a marathon on all 7 continents plus the North Pole

Joe Namath - the legendary quarterback is probably the most famous vegetarian football player. Inducted into the NFL Hall of Fame in 1985, he was also one of the best players, period.

Martina Navratilova - the Czech-born legend is one of the greatest tennis players of the 20th century. She won 18 Grand Slam singles titles and 31 doubles titles.

Dave Scott - holds the record for most Iron Man World Championship victories ever.

Billie Jean King - a longtime vegetarian, along with winning 12 Grand Slam titles and 16 doubles titles, she's famous for her Battle of the Sexes match, in which she defeated former men's Wimbledon champion Bobby Riggs.

Carl Lewis - wasn't always a vegetarian. But he eventually went even further: he adopted a vegan diet to prepare for the World Championships in 1991, where he says he ran the best meet of his life.

"Vegetarian involves weird fake meat"

I have honestly heard that bizarre statement as a reason why someone didn't want to try vegetarian food. I tried to point out to them that the food on their plate was ¾ vegetarian and only ¼ carnivore and that I seldom have any "fake meat".

I'm not going to even give this excuse any more page time.

"Plants have feelings too"

How scientific do you want to get?

Plants do not have a central nervous system. However, a central nervous system is not necessarily a requirement for a being to react to the environment. Even single-cell organisms can do this on a limited scale and there are a lot of plants that are known to react to their environment.

A central nervous system or a similar structure is necessary though for forming a representation of a certain state of the being (e.g. being touched) and further processing of that representation.

Now what is pain? In a nutshell you feel pain when nociceptors are activated (by various kind of stimuli: thermal, mechanical, chemical) and that activation is transmitted to your brain via neurons. Your brain then forms a representation of that activation et voilà you feel pain.

So, can plants feel pain? Possibly not. There are no mechanisms like the one described above present in plants. A simple reaction to the environment, as present in some plants, is not the same as pain.

If we assume for a moment that plants can feel pain, can they suffer? Even if plants can feel pain, by some mechanism that is unknown, it is still unlikely that they can suffer. Suffering requires a lot of higher cognitive functions, like emotions and memory. All the animal food that you eat have these functions.

"Lions kill animals"

And ...... that makes you a lion? Are you about to chase a gazelle, sink your teeth into it, rip it apart with your claws and eat it raw? I think I can safely say you'd rather get your food from the supermarket. Refer to chapter 4.

"We are at the top of the food chain"

Say that to a hungry lion then get back to me .... alternatively, refer to chapter 4.

"It won't make a difference, I'm just one person."

You will make the difference to the number of animals killed for your dining pleasure. That number is hard to calculate, but, think about it – by you introducing vegetarian meals into your life you certainly will not be party to some animals' death.

"I'd rather focus on people than animals"

I applaud you for this sentiment, however, there is no reason you can't do both. Vegetarianism, is simply a matter of choosing to eat plants rather than animals. You do not have to volunteer for anything. You do not have to donate money or time and you certainly do not have to travel to foreign lands or war-torn countries in order to "save" another sentient being. You just have to reach for the lentils in the supermarket, rather than reach for the chicken wings.

So there you have it. I think I've covered all your excuses, if not, feel free to get in touch with me. I'm sure I will have heard it before and will have an answer.

Just before you dash off to check out your pantry and head to the grocery store for some vegetarian items, just take a look at the next chapter to give yourself encouragement as to the company you will be in.

Chapter 12:

Vegetarians You May Know ... Well, probably not personally.

There are literally hundreds and hundreds of vegetarians dating right back to the ancient Greek poet and philosopher Empedocies and the founder of modern medicine, Hippocrates.

There's Leonardo de Vinci the artist, the poet Lord Byron and the writer Leo Tolstoy.

There are actors, writers, athletes, tennis players and boxers. Politicians and world leaders, revolutionaries and civil rights leaders. They are everywhere, in all countries, in all professions both past and present.

You can search the internet for a much more extensive list.

But to peak your interest .....

Rosanna Arquette
Alec Baldwin
Kim Basinger

Mayim Bialik
Russell Brand
Jessica Chastain
Ellen DeGeneres
Omar Epps
Corey Feldman
Richard Gere
Anne Hathaway
Paris Hilton
Jared Leto
Hayley Mills
Mary Tyler Moore
Leonard Nimoy
Sandra Oh
Ariana Huffington
Dennis Kucinich
Rosa Parks
Cesar Chavez
Julia "Butterfly" Hill
Andrew Bartlett, Australian Senator
Coretta Scott King
Martina Navratilova
Tony LaRussa
Hank Aaron
Jack LaLanne
Billie Jean King
Joe Namath
Scott Jurek
Bryan Adams
Travis Barker
Michael Franti (of Spearhead)
Alanis Morrisette

Sinead O'Connor
Prince
Alice Walker, writer
Allen Ginsberg, poet
Upton Sinclair
Clive Barker
Deepak Chopra, author and doctor
Kafka, writer
Louisa May Alcott
Mark Twain
William Blake
Voltaire
Leo Tolstoy
George Bernard Shaw
Percy Shelley
Steven Jobs
Dr. Ruth Bates
Casey Kasem
Don Imus
Chelsea Clinton
Jane Goodall
Uri Geller
John Mackey
Robin Quivers
Mr. Rogers
Yoko Ono
Vincent Van Gogh
Sir Isaac Newton
Leonardo Da Vinci
Ralph Waldo Emerson
Pythagoras
Plato

So, as you can see, you are in incredible company!!!!

I think that if the above can overcome any excuse they may have had, then so can you.

Hopefully I have managed to debunk your excuse and given you a good enough reason to at least give it a go, even if it is only one day a week.

There is just so much support out there, all you have to do is type your question into Google and you will get the answer.

Go online and see if there is a group close to where you live. Join an animal welfare organization and you'll certainly meet other vegetarians.

Just know that you are not alone. It really isn't hard to do ... just take the step and you will start a wonderful journey of discovery both in delicious tasting food and, more importantly, within yourself.

Finally.

Thank you for purchasing this book and taking the time to read through it. Did I manage to put your doubts into perspective? I certainly hope that I did, or at least, I have got you thinking.

Being vegetarian is a lifestyle and, usually, one that is chosen. However, like many things we choose to do, it does take practice and quite often the best results are when we start slowly. My one piece of advice to anyone thinking about going vegetarian is to begin with just one day a week.

Please check out my:
Website: www.thevegetariancenter.com
and
Blog:
www.thevegetariancenter.blogspot.co.nz

Happy Eating

The 2nd Book in the Good Life Series and a great companion to this one, is:

"How To Be Vegetarian – 7 easy steps to get started"

This book is also available on Amazon

Here's what one reader had to say about this book:
I've been trying to do vegetarian meals for a long time now but never knew where to start. To my surprise I do have many of the products, on the lists in this helpful book, in my pantry. I've had to cook separate meals for over 30 years now, because I have many food allergies, my husband does not. I also have found that I've had problems digesting red meat, and my husband is very fond of meat.... This book gave me ideas on how to add more healthy foods to my husband's "meat and potatoes meals." — **Bobbi**

What this book is NOT

It's not a recipe book
It's not a book telling you why
It's not telling to be full time vegetarian

What this book IS

It's a super easy "how to" book
It's full of tips and tricks to make life easy
It's got a great pantry list
It's even got your first shopping list

You can find this book by going to Amazon.com and typing in Fee O'Shea into the search box.

Get your FREE copy of "Getting You Started"

The Vegetarian Way
Getting You Started

Fee O'Shea

"The Vegetarian Way – Getting You Started" is an e-Book that you download from the internet. It is designed to give you a good start to the Vegetarian journey you are about to take.

It gives you a background into the new foods you'll be using as well as a couple of delicious, easy recipes in each category to get you started.

Type this link into your browser.

www.thevegetariancenter.com/the-vegetarian-way.php

About The Author

Author, consultant, vegan and animal welfare advocate, Fee O'Shea specializes in helping people step onto the path of vegetarianism.

Fee is a New Zealander who is a lover of great vegan food. After adopting a vegetarian lifestyle in the 90's she experimented with many different ingredients in order to create more appetizing and appealing food as New Zealand, at that time, was no where near embracing vegetarianism.

Early into the second decade of the 21st century, Fee had begun to learn about the welfare of farmed animals both overseas, but more importantly, within New Zealand. It was this knowledge of the farming industry that led her to adopt a vegan lifestyle.

She is actively involved with SAFE, a New Zealand organization which campaigns to stop factory farming along with other animal welfare issues, and she does what she can to help educate others to the benefits of adopting animal free living even if it is only for one day a week. She has an active blog where she takes great delight in venting her frustrations (in a humorous way), with animal welfare, lack of vegan choices, environment, short-sighted politicians and other things.

Fee has three children, two of whom are vegan, and two grandchildren. All her children have followed in her footsteps by being adventurous and creative great cooks and extremely conscious of animal welfare and planet earth.

Go to www.Amazon.com and type "Fee O'Shea" into the search box to find other books written by this author.

Resources

World Hunger:
features.peta2.com/making-the-connection/world-hunger.aspx

Environment change:
www.theguardian.com/environment/2012/apr/13/less-meat-prevent-climate-change

Nutrition:
www.webmd.com/food-recipes/guide/vitamins-and-minerals-good-food-sources

www.vegansociety.com/lifestyle/nutrition/sources-of-nutrition.aspx

Campaigns:
www.chickenout.tv/about-campaign/39-day-blog.html

www.porkbeinspired.com/towm_promo_heritage_page.aspx

www.fb.org/index.php?action=about.history

www.adage.com/article/special-report-the-advertising-century/ad-age-advertising-century-top-100-campaigns/140918/

www.sourcewatch.org/index.php/Meat_%26_Da
iry_industry

Sports:
www.mnn.com/food/healthy-eating/photos/9-
superstar-athletes-who-dont-eat-meat/fueled-
by-vegetables

Science:
www.thenakedscientists.com

www.reddit.com/r/vegan/comments/1ede41/do
_plants_have_feelings_too/

Also:

The pork industry in N.Z. and USA.
The beef industry in N.Z. USA and Europe.
The chicken industry both for eggs and eating in
N.Z. USA and Europe.
The dairy industry in N.Z. and USA.

Variety of meat processing practices.

Medical journals of USA, UK and N.Z.

Printed in Great Britain
by Amazon